GRADE 1 SCIENCE:
FOR CURIOUS KIDS

BABY PROFESSOR

EDUCATION KIDS

ANiMALS
& WHAT
THEY EAT

MONKEYS EAT
BANANAS

HORSES EAT CORN AND GRASS

DOGS EAT BONES

FiSHES EAT WORMS

TURTLES EAT
WORMS & FRUITS

ELEPHANTS EAT FRUITS

SHEEPS EAT
GRASS

MiCE EAT
CHEESE

RABBiTS EAT
CARROTS

MY BODY
PARTS

STOMACH

ARM

CHiN

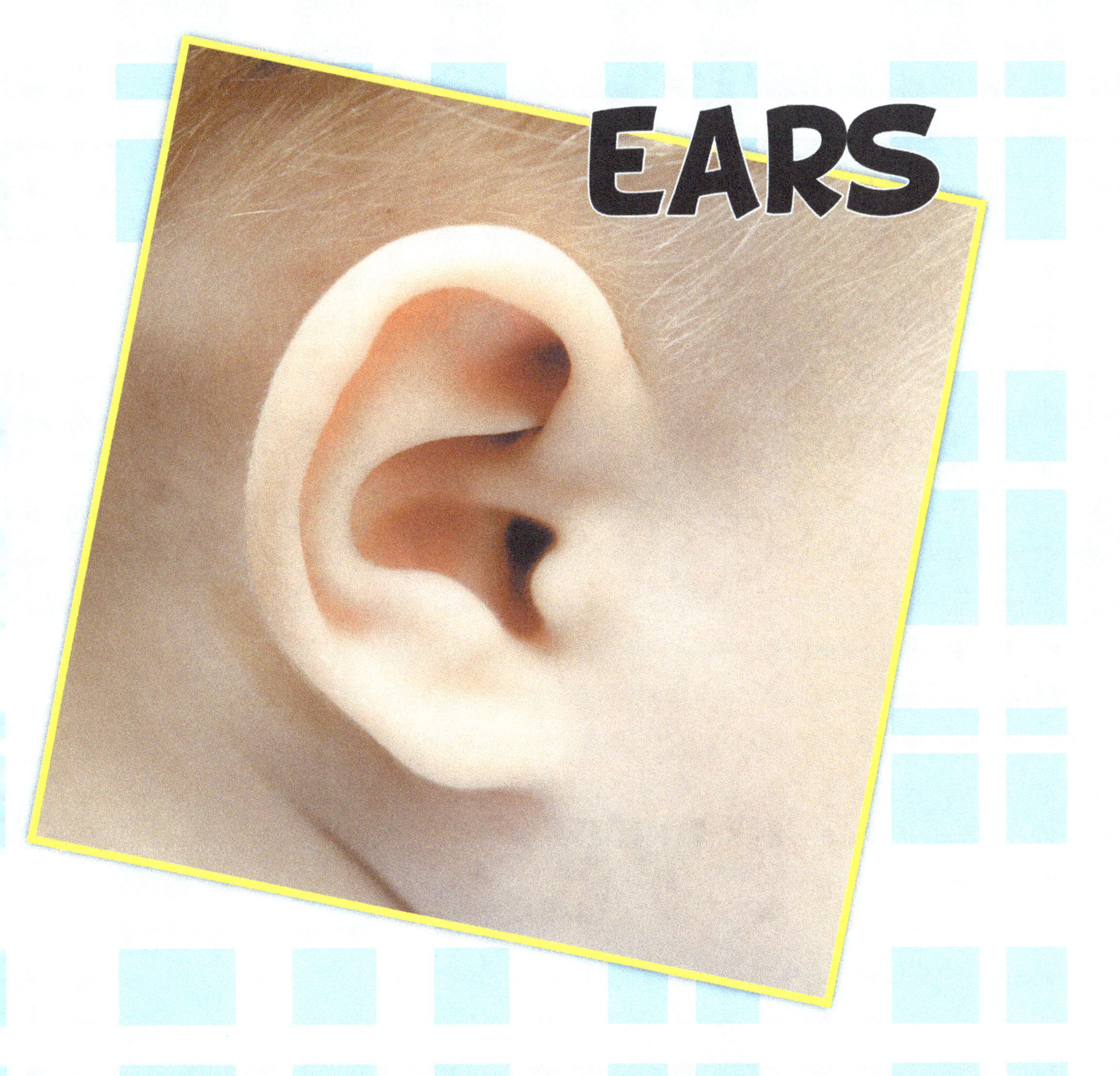
EARS

EYES

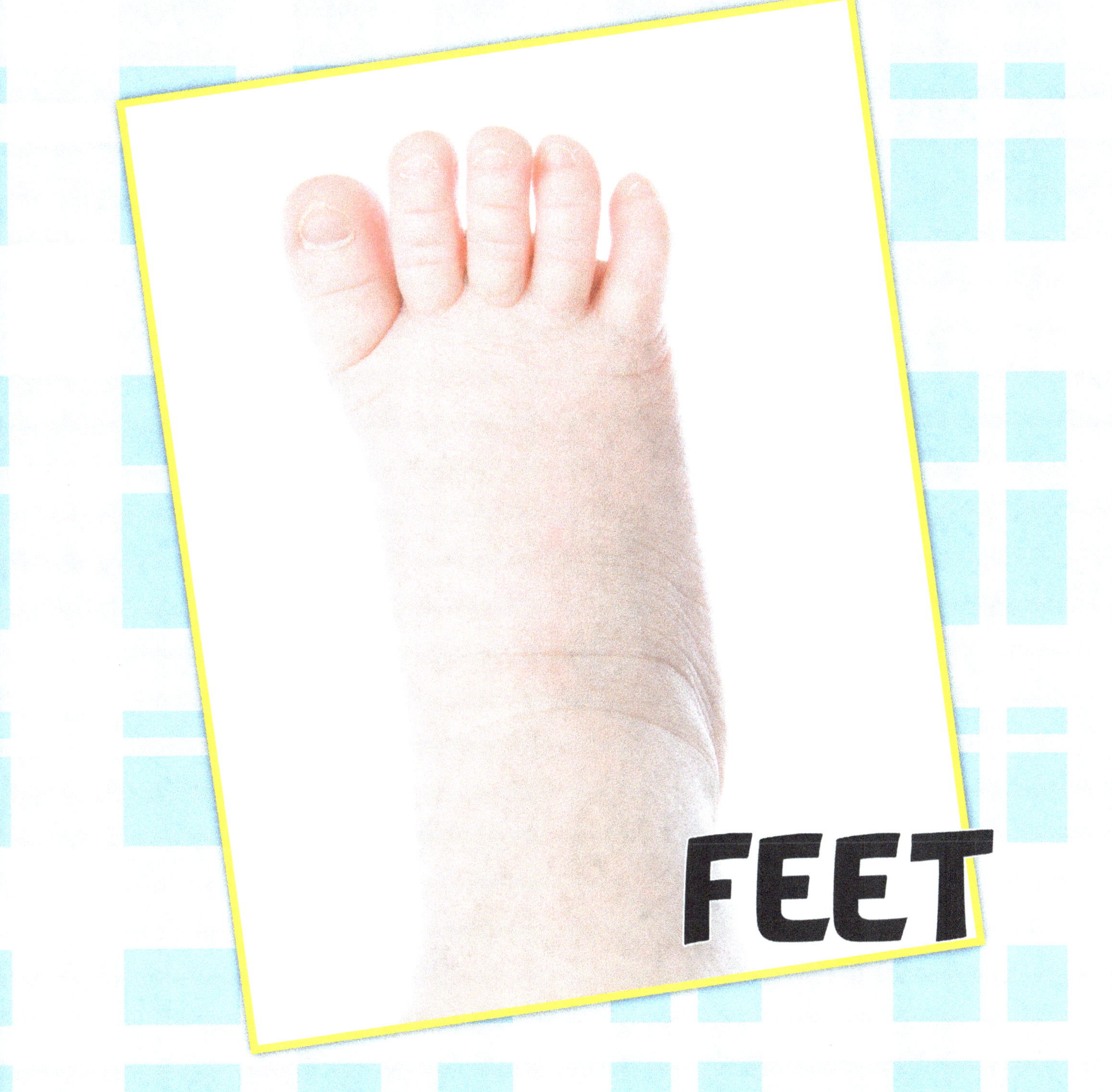

FEET

KNEE

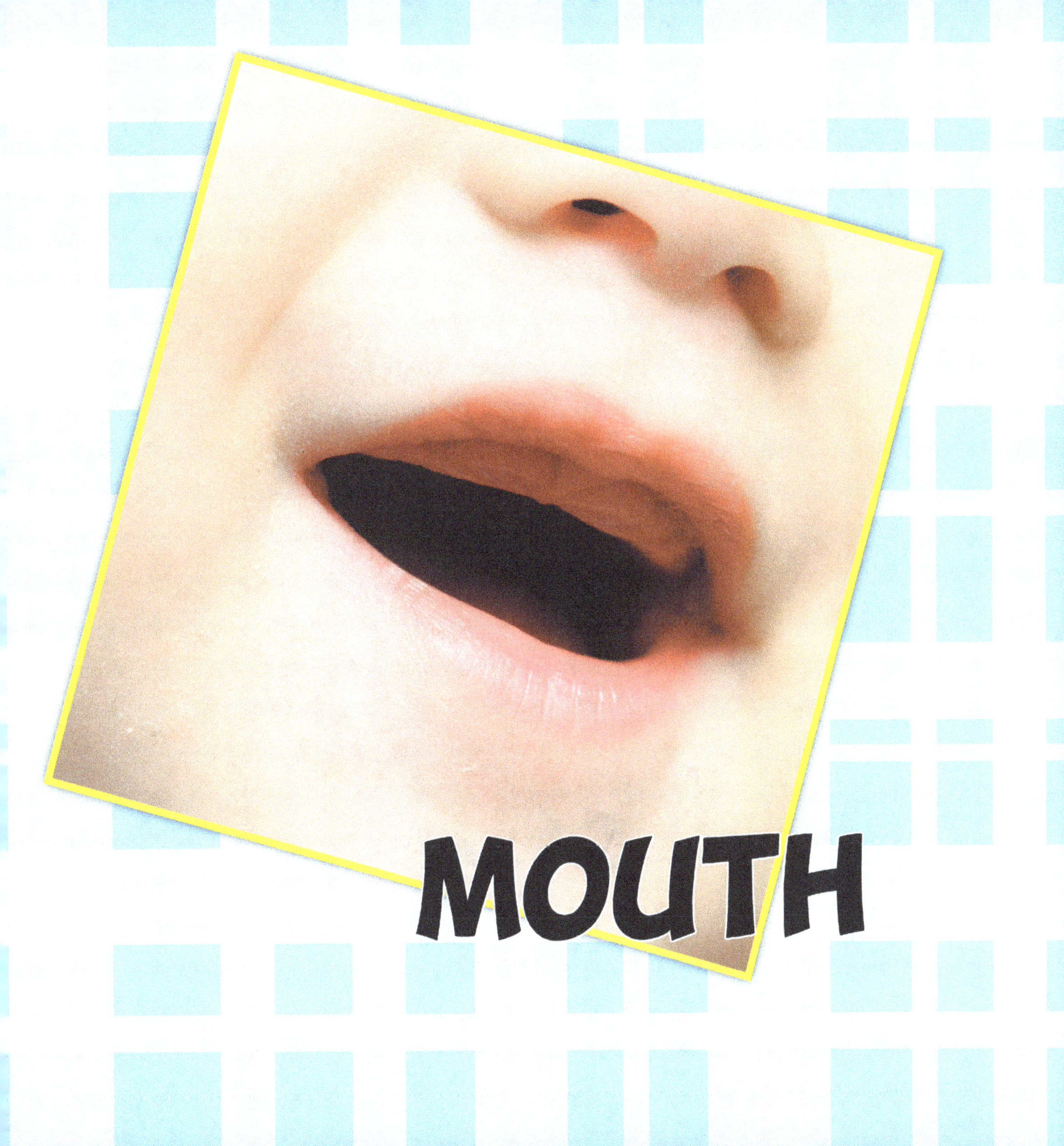
MOUTH

NECK

COMMON
"WHY DO
i'S?"

WHY DOES MY NOSE RUN?

Reason: You may have a cold or the flu; you may have allergies; you're maybe crying; or it's cold outside.

WHY DO MY EYES WATER?

Reason: The tears from watering eyes help protect your eyes. By keeping them moist and washing out dust and other foreign stuff that gets in there.

WHY DO I SWEAT?

Reason: When your body gets hotter, your brain doesn't like it — it wants your body to stay cool and comfortable.

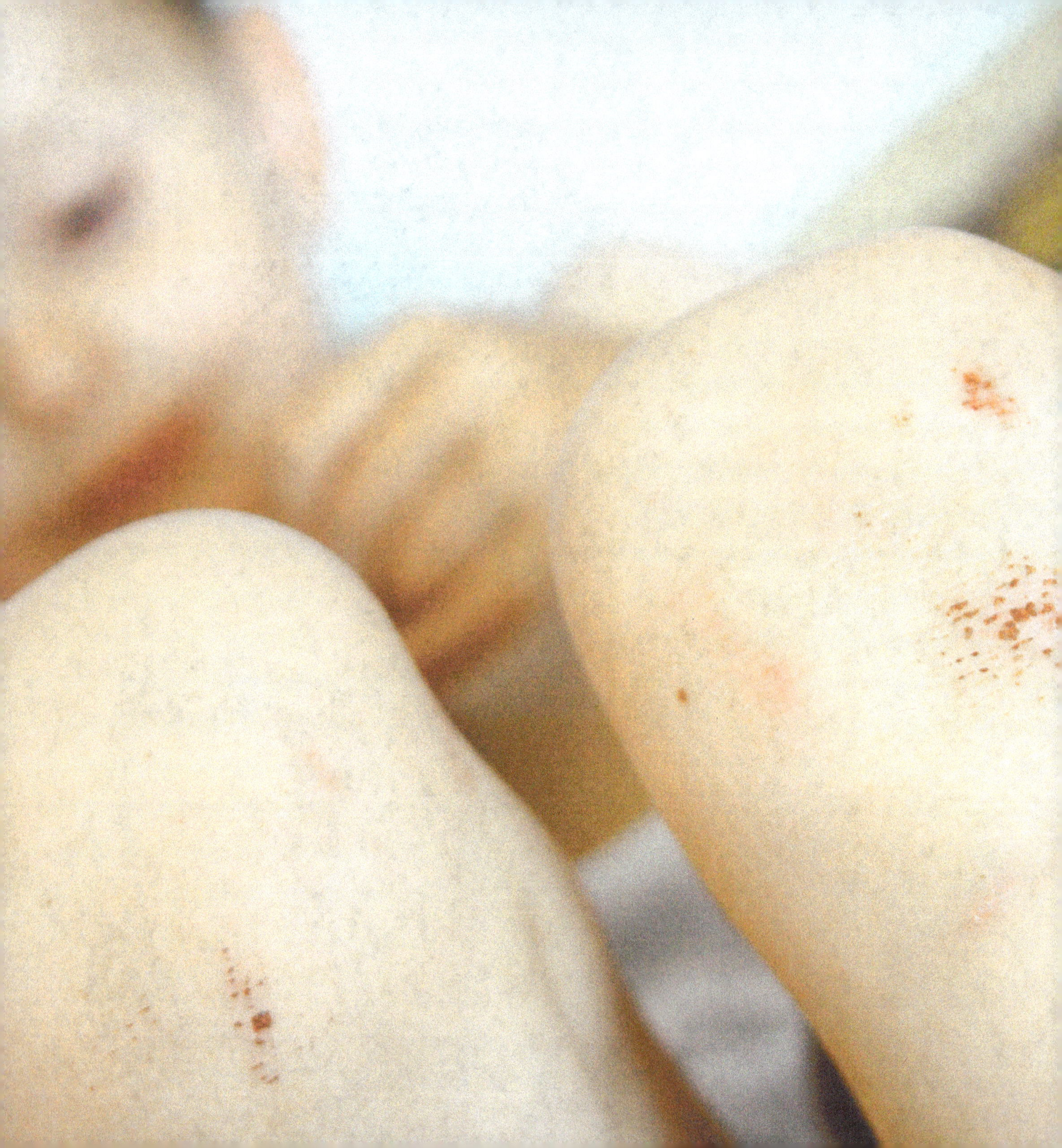

WHY DO I GET BRUISES?

Reason: This is because the soft tissues of your body have been bumped.